SECOND EDITION

Storybook 14

The
Ball Book

by Sue Dickson

Illustrations by Norma Portadino, Jean Hamilton, Chip Neville and Kerstin Upmeyer

Printed in the United States of America

Copyright © 1998 Sue Dickson
International Learning Systems of North America, Inc.
St. Petersburg, FL 33716

ISBN: 1-56704-524-3 (Volume 14)

C D E F G H I J K L M N—CJK—05 04 03 02 01 99

Table of Contents
Raceway Step 28

Vocabulary

1. all

2. fall

3. hall

4. wall

5. small

6. call

7. called

8. ball

basket ball

9. basketball

The basketball coach was going to pick the team today. All the kids wanted to be on it. They waited in the hall to see Coach Dobbs. Some sat on benches and some leaned on the wall.

The tall kids were sure they would be picked.

4

The not-so-tall
kids hoped to be on the
team too.

Nick was not-so-tall. He
was small, but he played
basketball very well. He
wished Coach Dobbs
would pick him to be on
the team.

5

Soon it was Nick's turn to see the coach.

Mr. Walter Dobbs

Coach

"Come on in, Nick," he called. "I am glad to say you made the team. You are small, but you are fast. We can't **all** be tall."

"Thank you, sir !" Nick said. He grinned. "This is going to be a wonderful fall. We will all do our best for the team !"

The End

No War

Vocabulary

1. warm

2. swarmed

3. war

4. toward

5. reward

6. wart

7. warned

<u>Story Word</u>

8. who

There was a sailor who
had no fear,
And he lived not-so-far
from here.
His boat wrecked in a
sudden storm.
He floated toward a land
that's warm.

Safe on the beach
the man lay down.
Soon little natives
swarmed from the town.
One native warned
"Just hear that roar!
Hurry men, get set for war!"

"This giant we must tie
up tight,
So he can't get loose
tonight !
Do you suppose that there
could be
A good reward for you
and me ?"

They poked the giant
on his wart !
He sat up with an
awful snort !

He towered way up in
the sky.
They never saw a man
so high !

The giant said, "Just treat
me right
And you will never have
to fight.
I will be a pal for you,
and I will help in all
you do."
The natives now are glad
once more.
They really did not want
a war !

The End

14

Mrs. Hodges' Surprise

Vocabulary

1. Hodges
2. Ridge Park
3. dodge
4. wedged
5. sledge
6. midget
7. budge
8. ledge
9. budget
10. nudged
11. trudged
12. hedge
13. edge
14. bridge
15. fudge
16. pledge
17. judge

The boys missed Mrs. Hodges! She had gone to Park Ridge. She had been away for weeks now. She always let Ray and David play dodge-ball in her yard. She was a very nice neighbor.

"Let's fix up her yard," said Ray and David.

Ray and David ran to get the lawn mower. Ray lifted the latch of the tool shed. There was the mower wedged way in the back.

Ray lifted the tools out of the way. "This sledge hammer is no midget," he said. "It weighs a ton !"

At last Ray and David cleared a space to get to the mower.

Ray grabbed the handle.
It would not budge! It
was caught under the
window ledge. David took
hold of the wheels. He
nudged the mower away
from the window.

"Here we go!" said Ray.

19

Then David and Ray
trudged back with their
tools.

When they reached Mrs.
Hodges' yard, Ray trimmed
the hedge. David cut the
grass to the edge of the
fence.

20

The boys had just finished when Mrs. Hodges drove over the bridge. She was soon home in her driveway.

"What a nice surprise !" said Mrs. Hodges. "I really missed you boys while I was away. I have a surprise for you, too !" Mrs. Hodges gave the boys a big box of fudge.

"Thank you, and welcome home !" the boys replied.

It was nice to have a neighbor like Mrs. Hodges. Ray and David were glad they had fixed up her yard. They made a pledge. They would do Mrs. Hodges' yard every week.

The End

Vocabulary

1. Sue
2. flue
3. hue
4. glue
5. true
6. clue
7. due

<u>Story Words</u>

val en tine
8. valentine

fire light
9. firelight

fire place
10. fireplace

Feb ru ary
11. February

sil ver
12. silver

mail box
13. mailbox

mail man
14. mailman

dif fer ent
15. different

16. friends

17. guess

24

Sue helped her mother open the fireplace flue. They made a nice warm fire.

"February 14 will be here soon," said Sue. "I must make my valentines today."

25

Soon Sue started to make them. She had blue and silver paper. The firelight gave the silver paper a different hue.

"This silver paper looks blue!" said Sue.

26

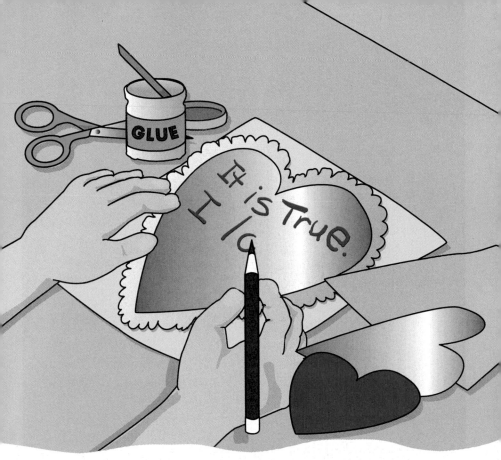

Sue used glue to add a
little silver paper and
some lace to each
valentine. Then she
wrote: "It is true, I love
you" on each one.

Sue did not put her name on the valentines, but she gave this clue: 19-21-5. Can you guess who ?

A B C D E F G H I J K L M N
O P Q R S T U V W X Y Z

The mailman was due to come soon. Sue had to hurry to the mailbox with her valentines.

Sue had fun sending pretty valentines to her friends.

The End

Uncle Max

Vocabulary

1. Max
2. fix
3. box
4. ax
5. wax
6. next
7. mix
8. ox
9. fox
10. six

11. relax

<u>Story Words</u>

12. any thing
    anything

13. a while
    awhile

14. fin ish
    finish

15. finished

16. easy

17. sure

30

Tony loved to help his Uncle Max. Uncle Max could fix anything. He could do so many things.

31

Tony helped his Uncle Max make a tool box,

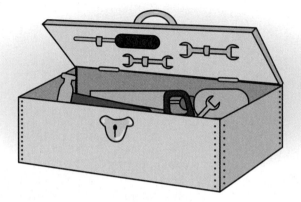

sharpen an ax,

Take care, Tony !

**WOW !
That sure looks like
a sharp edge !**

and even clean and wax
his car.

"What will we do next,
Uncle Max ?" asked Tony.

Uncle Max said, "Tony, do you think you could mix this paint for me? It is thick and lumpy."

Tony was glad to do something by himself. He said, "I am strong. I will try." So Tony started mixing the paint.

Directions for Mixing Latex Paint
Start with a smooth flat stick, then
stir in a circular motion, fixing lumps.
Mixture will become satiny and smooth,
and of an excellent texture.

After awhile Uncle Max looked to see if the paint was mixed.

"Well," said Uncle Max, "I would say you are as strong as an ox and as smart as a fox! With such good help, I can be finished before six o' clock!"

Tony sat down to relax a bit. Tony thought about Uncle Max. He said the nicest things !

Out loud, Tony said, "Do you really think I am as strong as an ox, Uncle Max ?"

"And as smart as a fox !" said Uncle Max.

36

The End

The Jewel Thief

Vocabulary

1. chief
2. believes
3. thief

brief case
4. briefcase

5. pier
6. priest
7. niece
8. fierce
9. yield

10. shield
11. relief

Green field
12. Greenfield

Story Words

13. police
14. sure
15. full
16. read
17. put

37

Jill was reading The Greenfield News to her mom. Jill said, "The Chief of Police believes a thief stole a briefcase full of jewels from the Greenfield Pier."

Jill went on reading...

Jewel Thief at Pier

A priest and his niece, who were on the pier yesterday, saw a big car leave the pier at a fierce speed.

"It went through a yield sign," said the priest. "It made so much dust, I had to shield my face for a brief time. I did not get the license plate number."

The

jum

Wh

fox

dog

fox

l

The

ju

Jill said, "I bet it will be a relief to the chief when the briefcase is found."

"Yes," said Mom. "We can be sure our police chief will catch that thief !"

The End

A Bear's Steak

Vocabulary

1. **break**

2. **steak**

3. **great**

modified $\bar{a}$ sound

4. **bear**

5. **pear**

At break of day
Sat Little Dan

Cooking his steak
In a frying pan.

Out of the woods came a
great big bear !

Dan rushed up the tree and dined on a pear !

The End

A Breath of Spring

Vocabulary

1. weather
2. Heather
3. heaven
4. ready
5. sweaters
6. leather
7. steady
8. heavy
9. wealthy
10. read
11. health
12. instead
13. bread
14. feather
15. head
16. dead
17. thread
18. breath

"The weather is perfect,"
said Heather. "Not a
cloud in heaven. Spring
must be here at last!"

"Let's get ready to go out
in our boat," said Gus.

OK, I'm ready!

Let's go!

Me, too!

"Fine," said Mother. "Put on your sweaters or your leather jackets. It is still cool."

Mother tied a scarf on her head.

"Hold the boat steady while we get in," said Heather.

"OK," said Gus. "I will haul this up slowly. It is heavy."

"Look ! Those men are getting a fish !" said Mom.

"I read that eating fish is good for your health," said Gus.

"Yes, and we may have some fish for dinner if you catch any," Mom said, "with fresh bread and butter, too !"

Just then a sea gull flew over the boat. A white feather *floated down* onto Heather's head. "Look! A feather from heaven!" yelled Heather.

50

"Look at the crab !"
yelled Heather. "Let's try
to get it !"

Gus picked up the crab
net and stretched to get
the crab.

"Oh, it is dead,
Heather. I will throw it
back in," he said.

Gus had a button. It
caught on a nail. It
was hanging by a thread.
"Yank it off, Gus. You
may put it in your
sweater pocket," said
Mom. "We will fix
it later."

Then Mom looked up to heaven. She took a deep breath and said, "This is so good for your health ! Let's do this every day !"

The End

The Search for the Pearls

Vocabulary

eør=er

1. heard
2. search
3. searched
4. pearl
5. learn
6. learned
7. Earl
8. early
9. earned
10. earth

f–ves

11. thief
12. thieves
13. wife
14. wives
15. leaf
16. leaves
17. loaf
18. loaves
19. knife
20. knives

Story Word

21. fierce

54

"Have you ever heard the story <u>The Search for the Pearls</u> ?" asked Grandfather.

Earl said, "No, I never heard that one."

Will you tell it to me, please Grandpa ?

"When we finish raking these leaves, I will tell you," said Grandfather.

Grandfather and Earl raked up every leaf.

Grandmother called from
the porch, "Come in and
I will cut a slice of
bread for you."

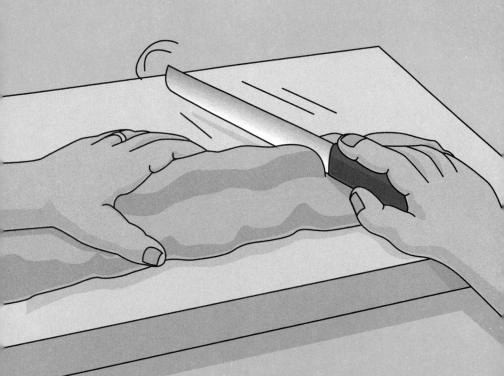

"You have earned it. I just baked three loaves," she said.

Grandfather and Earl ran into the house.

Grandmother had a sharp knife. She cut the loaf of bread for them. 57

"This is good bread, dear," said Grandfather. "Of all the wives on earth, you are the best wife !"

"And **you** are the best husband," said Grand-mother. "Thank you for sharpening my knives."

58

When they finished eating, Grandfather began his story:

"Once upon a time, there were two brothers, Sam and Ben. They went around the earth to search for pearls. Their wives went with them."

"They learned that a pirate ship had sunk in the sea nearby. On the ship there was a huge chest of fine pearls !"

"Early one morning, Sam and Ben and their wives set out to search for the pearls. They searched and searched for days and days. At last they **found** the chest ! They hauled up the chest of pearls from the sea !"

The Early Bird

Grandfather went on: "Then Sam and Ben and their wives dove back down to search for **more** pearls. When they came back up, guess what they saw?"

"Thieves were going off
with their chest of pearls !"
"Oh, no !" they yelled.
"Let's go after them."
"As they chased after the
thieves, a fierce storm
came up !"

"The thieves' ship sank !
The sea was so deep, no
one ever found that chest of
pearls again ! Those pearls
may still be there today !"

"Wow !" said Earl. "I'd
like to go search for them !"

"Maybe you **will** some
day !" said Grandfather
with a smile.

The End